Original Cover drawn in class by Violet

Violet Kane, 9 Years old

Publisher

10-10-10 Publishing

10-10-10 Publishing
Markham, ON
Canada

Printed and bound in Canada

Lilly is Quiet
Copyright © 2020 by Violet Kane
All rights reserved.
ISBN: 978-1-77277-374-3

First edition - November 2020

All rights reserved. No portion of this book may be reproduced mechanically, electronically, or by any other means, including photocopying, without permission of the publisher or author except in the case of brief quotations embodied in critical articles and reviews. It is illegal to copy this book, post it to a website, or distribute it by any other means without permission from the publisher or author.

Limits of Liability and Disclaimer of Warranty
The author and publisher shall not be liable for your misuse of the enclosed material. This book is strictly for informational and educational purposes only.

Warning - Disclaimer
The purpose of this book is to educate and entertain. The author and/or publisher do not guarantee that anyone following these techniques, suggestions, tips, ideas, or strategies will become successful. The author and/or publisher shall have neither liability nor responsibility to anyone with respect to any loss or damage caused, or alleged to be caused, directly or indirectly by the information contained in this book.

Publisher

Markham, ON
Canada

Printed and bound in Canada

"Violet has written a wonderful story. I enjoyed it a lot."

Robert Munsch,
New York Times Bestselling Children's Author

In Memory of

My Aunt Heather MacLeod
Who definitely had one fun and amazing voice
And dedicated
To those who seek to find a voice of their own

Lilly was a very happy cat.
But, she didn't know how to express that
for a long time.
Lilly hardly ever got what she wanted because,
nobody could hear her

One day Lilly went to the park and saw her friend Andrew, he asked, "Lilly, do you want to go first on the slide?" Lilly responded, "Yes, I do" in a very quiet tone. Andrew couldn't hear her so he went first. Lilly's face turned blood red.

Lilly wasn't always this quiet. She had a bad experience with music class in kindergarten. Her and Andrew were sitting on the carpet, whispering about after school when suddenly they heard their music teacher scream, "HEY!" Lilly blushed and her palms sweat. All of the other children set their eyes on Lilly and Andrew. The music teacher's face was now a dark, dark red.
Lilly's face turned completely pale.
Ever since then, Lilly was quiet.

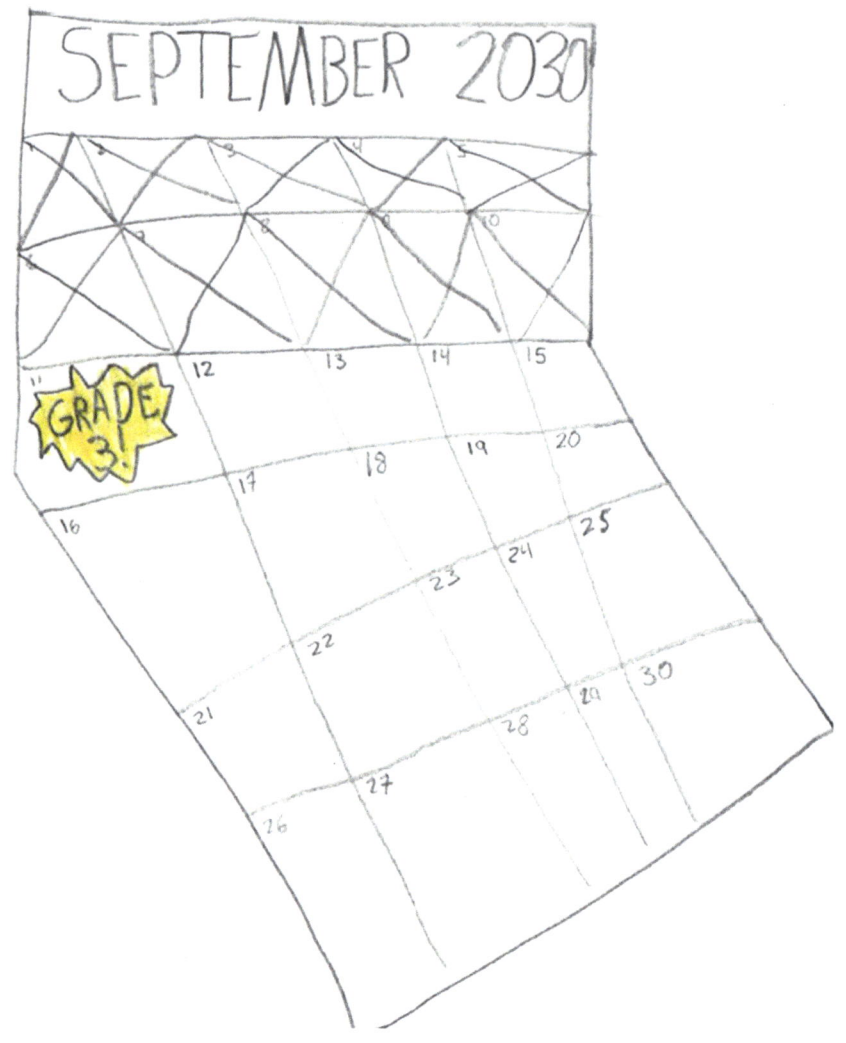

Sweat trickled slowly down Lilly's back. It was the first day of grade 3! She was very nervous because Lilly knew that one of the grade 3 teachers was Mrs. Elephant, the kindergarten music teacher.

When Lilly got to school, she was relieved to see that her teacher was Ms. Giraffe. The first words that Ms. Giraffe said to the class were, "Hello everyone, what are your names?", "Marthia, Fred, Julia, Andrew," said all of the students loudly. Lilly said, "I'm Lilly", in a very quiet tone.

That day at lunch, Lilly strolled over to the cafeteria and asked if she could have a burger and fries very quietly. The lunch lady couldn't hear her so Lilly got meatloaf and potatoes. Lilly's stomach growled like a tiger as the lunch lady scooped her unwanted lunch.

As Lilly slowly emerged at an empty lunch table, the grade 6's started to laugh at Lilly. "I didn't want this", Lilly thought as she gulped down her meal.

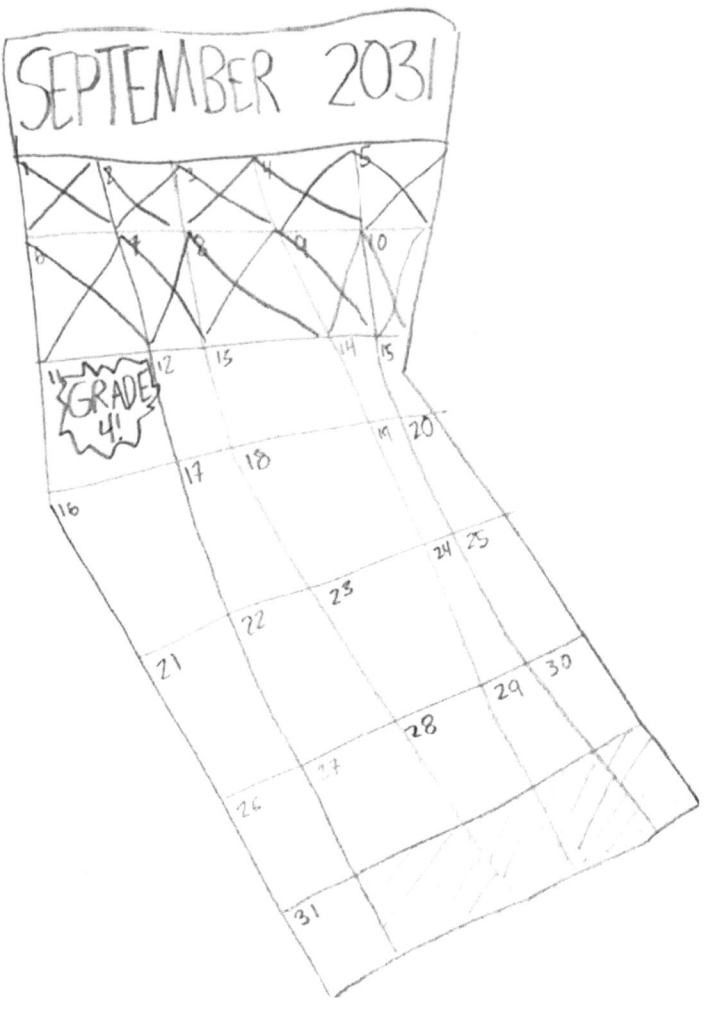

Now, Lilly was in grade 4. This year she felt the least confident of all the years that she was in school because Lilly knew that every Monday, the grade 4's went to see the grade 1's for buddies. The first day of school was Monday; Lilly started to quiver.

Once Lilly got into the classroom, her new teacher Mrs. Skunk announced, "Today we are going to see the first graders!". "Yay!" shouted all of the students except Lilly. "Oh, no." thought Lilly.

When the grade 4's got to the classroom of the grade 1's, Lilly picked a partner named Ava. Ava shouted, "Hi, Lilly." Lilly whispered back, "Hello Ava." They got straight to work. All of the talking that Lilly did was whispering. But, what Lilly didn't notice was that everytime Ava talked, she got a bit quieter.

Once buddies was over, Lilly was shocked to see that Ava's powerful and loud hello, turned into a soft whisper, "Bye Lilly, I'm quiet now too." Lilly responded, "Bye Ava," in a very quiet tone, "Uh oh" Lilly thought as she strolled out the door with the rest of her class. After that, all of the grade 1's started to copy Lilly and Ava. Then the kindergarteners, grade 2's, and grade 3's! Even the older students started to become quiet as well! Lilly knew that she urgently needed to do something.

The next week was summer vacation. During the summer, Lilly changed, she felt different. Like something clicked inside of her. On the first day of grade 5, Lilly made a commitment, she would be louder, and stand up for herself from now on.

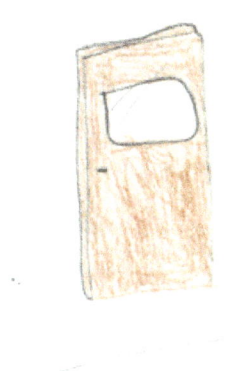

Lilly proudly walked into her grade 5 portable, and when the teacher asked, "What are your names?" "Andrew, Julia, Lilly..." said all of the students loudly. Now everybody could hear Lilly. At lunch Lilly got the lunch that she wanted, and she sat with all of her other classmates, Lilly had a perfect split lip grin for the whole day.

After school that day, Andrew and Julia invited Lilly to the park. She could see that after Andrew touched his forehead his hand was wet. Andrew really wanted Lilly to go to the park. Lilly agreed to go to the park. They had a long peaceful walk to the park, and on the way, Lilly talked more than normal, and louder than normal as well.

At the park, Andrew and Julia let Lilly decide which apparatus she wanted to use first. Now, they heard Lilly and she wanted to go on the slide, Andrew wanted monkey bars, and Julia the swing. From that day on, Lilly was louder everywhere she went. She had lots of friends and everyone could hear her.

THE END

ABOUT THE AUTHOR:

Violet Kane wrote and illustrated "Lilly is Quiet" in class during her third-grade creative writing class. She loves writing and performing plays and stories with her siblings and cousins to the delight of her family. Violet also loves going up to her family cottage with family and friends, training dogs, jet skiing, swimming, badminton, planning events, making TikToks, animals, tennis and skiing. She lives in Toronto with her family including well loved Cava-doodle Scout and cat Cutie Pie Junior.

ACKNOWLEDGEMENTS

I would first like to thank my friends Charlotte, Chloe, Katie, Rachel, Lauren, Matthew, Ryan, Sienna and the rest of my other friends for being kind and supportive.

Also, a huge thanks to my third-grade teacher Mark King for teaching me the structure of books and how to write them. He is thoughtful, wise, kind, understanding and hardly ever raises his voice. That's not something that you would normally see in a teacher. Without Mr. King none of this would've happened and I am extremely grateful that I got to be in his class. So, thank-you Mr. King.

A big thanks to my family for supporting and helping me every step of the way. My mom, dad, sister Sara and brother Joe were amazing support and they helped make it happen.

I would also like to acknowledge the rest of my family including cousins, (Melodie, Kiah, Sage, Amy, Laura, Stephanie, Brendan and Matthew), aunts, (Heather, Bev, Lydia, Helen, Shelly, Carol and Kathie), uncles, (Tyler, Terry, John, Rob, and Tom), and my grandparents, (Gigi, Grandma and Zaidy) for encouraging me.

ACKNOWLEDGEMENTS (cont.)

Also, a huge thanks to all the teachers that I've had in the past, and still have now. First, a big thanks to my kindergarten teacher Nancy Willoughby for teaching me how to spell and write full sentences. Then a huge thanks to Jason Chong, my first-grade teacher for teaching me descriptive sentences using adjectives, verbs and nouns. Then, a big thanks to my second-grade teacher, Susan Thurow for helping me learn paragraphs and complet sentences. Also, a giant thanks to my fourth grade and third-grade coding teacher Mrs. Millan for being fun, nice and for teaching me how to write narratives and use better grammar. I would also like to thank Meera Jane for being the best and funniest French teacher ever.

Testimonials from my teachers:

Kindergarten teacher:
"Violet Kane's story captures the experience of those who travel through the world in a quiet yet thoughtful way. The experiences of her main character Lilly are told with authenticity and compassion. The reader can feel Lilly's frustration when she is unable to communicate what she wants — whether it is a turn on the slide or a favourite meal at the cafeteria. In the end we are cheering for Lilly as she learns to speak out and find her own way at school!"
—Ms. Nancy Willoughby

Grade 1 teacher:
"A tour de force!"
—Mr. Chong

Grade 2 teacher:
"I had the pleasure of being Violet's grade two teacher and even at the young age of 7 she showed a love of reading and a passion for writing. As a grade two student, Violet wrote a beautiful personal narrative about her trip to Florida. It was full of rich details and descriptions. I am so happy that Violet has continued her journey as an author. I so enjoyed reading her latest book and I look forward to reading many more!"
—Ms. Susan Thurow

Testimonials from my teachers:

Grade 3 teacher:

"Violet Kane is an exceptionally thoughtful and creative writer, especially for someone of her young age. She infuses her work with heartfelt lessons from her life and the joyful enthusiasm of youth. Lilly is Quiet is a semi-autobiographical story of a young student's journey of self-discovery and personal growth after a traumatic experience with a teacher. The story is essential reading for adults to understand the power of the words they speak to children and for the children to understand that they needn't be limited by the opinion of their elders."

-Mr. Mark King

www.ingramcontent.com/pod-product-compliance
Lightning Source LLC
Chambersburg PA
CBHW061051090426
42740CB00002B/116